HORACE DAVIS

THIRD SERIES
IX-X

AMERICAN CONSTITUTIONS

The Relations of the Three Departments
as Adjusted by a Century

Elibron Classics
www.elibron.com

Elibron Classics series.

ISBN 1-4212-1054-1 (paperback)
ISBN 1-4212-1053-3 (hardcover)

This Elibron Classics Replica Edition is an unabridged facsimile of the edition published in 1885 by John Hopkins University, Baltimore.

IX-X

AMERICAN CONSTITUTIONS

JOHNS HOPKINS UNIVERSITY STUDIES
IN
HISTORICAL AND POLITICAL SCIENCE

HERBERT B. ADAMS, Editor

History is past Politics and Politics present History—*Freeman*

THIRD SERIES

IX-X

AMERICAN CONSTITUTIONS

The Relations of the Three Departments as Adjusted by a Century

BY HORACE DAVIS
San Francisco, California

BALTIMORE
N. MURRAY, PUBLICATION AGENT, JOHNS HOPKINS UNIVERSITY
September and October, 1885

THE FRIEDENWALD CO., PRINTERS,
BALTIMORE.

CONTENTS.

I.

PAGE.

INTRODUCTION 7

Colonial Governments 9

II.

CONSTITUTIONS OF THE REVOLUTIONARY PERIOD 12

Warnings of the Revolutionary Statesmen 14

III.

MODERN STATE CONSTITUTIONS 17

Limitations upon Legislation 18

Southern Confederacy 21

IV.

THE FEDERAL GOVERNMENT 22

Opposition to a Strong Judiciary 24

Balance of Powers 25

Encroachments of Congress 28

Political Riders 29

President Hayes and Congress 30

Appointment and Removal of Officers 32

To the Victors belong the Spoils 33

President Jackson's Extraordinary Claims 35

Congress and Andrew Johnson 39

The Veto Power 40

V.

THE JUDICIARY 44

The Revolutionary Constitutions 46

The Modern Constitutions 47

Relations of the Judiciary to the Executive 49

Interference with the Independence of the Courts 52

Great Power of American Courts 55

Resistance to the Claims of the Courts 57

Conclusion 60

The Courts the Conscience of the People 61

APPENDIX 65

Tabulated Comparison of Modern State Constitutions 67

AMERICAN CONSTITUTIONS.

I.

All the nations sharing our form of civilization make a three-fold division of the functions of government into legislative, executive and judicial departments. On the proper separation and independence of these departments rest in a great measure the liberties of the people. The union of all these departments under one authority constitutes a despotism: while in different and independent hands they form checks upon each other against usurpation. To adjust carefully the balance of these powers, to define their fields of action, to bestow on each independence and a power of self-defense, is the supreme effort of modern governmental science. Our fathers inherited from Great Britain the idea of this three-fold division of government, and introduced it, although imperfectly, in their early constitutions.

My object in this paper is to present a brief historic sketch of the change in the relations of these departments which has been silently going on in the United States for the past century. In the State Governments, the numerous alterations in their constitutions since 1790 have steadily enlarged the powers of the Executive and cramped and limited the functions of the Legislatures. But, on the other hand, in the Federal Government, without constitutional amendments in this particular, Congress, with the natural aggressiveness of popular bodies, has encroached somewhat upon the field of Executive power; while everywhere, in both National and State Governments, the Judiciary has gained vastly in power and importance. Let us trace these changes, beginning with the State Constitutions.

There have been substantially three distinct strata of government in the thirteen old colonies, each stratum quite marked in its character, though having many things in common with the others: first, the colonial governments; second, the revolutionary constitutions adopted during the War of Independence; third, the modern forms of government. During the first period, "the good old colony times when we all lived under the King," nearly all the colonies were ruled by Royal Governors, representing in miniature the dignity and power of his British Majesty. The Governor appointed all the officers, including the Judiciary; he had command of the land and naval forces, and possessed an unqualified veto on all legislation. The exceptions to this type will be noted hereafter. In the second period, the people, stung by the exactions of an irresponsible executive, nervous with fear of one-man rule, rushed to the other extreme, and placed all real power in the hands of the Legislature springing directly from the people. The balance was again disturbed, the pendulum swung clear to the other end of the arc. The power of the Legislature in many States was almost as absolute as that of the British Parliament, without its conservative elements. Wise men trembled for the permanence of the government, and Madison and Jefferson have left us the record of their fears. But the calm judgment of the people prevailed over their alarms. Slowly they rebuilt their hasty work, readjusting and poising the great structure. This has been the work of the third period, to balance the powers of the government; to limit and define the functions of the three great departments, and establish their independence within proper boundaries, so that I believe our State Constitutions are to-day as a whole the most perfect framework of government, for men living in a democracy, that human skill has ever devised. Returning to the first period, a brief notice is demanded of

The Colonial Governments.

In the first volume of Story's Commentaries on the Constitution can be found a sketch of them; Bancroft's United States gives fuller details. Story divides them into three classes:

1st. Charter Governments, including Massachusetts, Rhode Island and Connecticut.

2d. Proprietary Governments, to which belong Pennsylvania, Delaware and Maryland.

3d. Provincial Governments, comprising the remaining seven colonies.

Each colony had a Legislature elected by the people, suffrage being usually limited to the freeholders. Pennsylvania and Georgia had only a single legislative body, but the remaining eleven colonies had each a higher branch, usually called the Council, which was appointed by the Governor, except in Massachusetts, Rhode Island and Connecticut, where it was chosen, directly or indirectly, by the people. The Governor was appointed by the Crown or the Proprietaries, except in Rhode Island and Connecticut. These two colonies enjoyed the exceptional privilege of choosing their own Executive. Thus the Governors in eleven colonies were independent of the people, while their powers were very extensive. They were commanders-in-chief of the armed forces by land and by sea; they appointed all officers military and civil, including judges; they appointed the Council and could suspend it; they could assemble or dissolve the Legislature; they had an unqualified veto on all laws, except in Pennsylvania; and they all had the power of pardoning offences. Besides these broad restrictions on popular government, the Crown claimed the right to veto all laws and to entertain appeals from the Courts of last resort in the colonies. In Rhode Island and Connecticut, however, under their peculiarly liberal institutions, the Legislatures appointed all officers, civil and military, and the Governors possessed no veto power; while in these two colonies and Maryland, the laws needed not to be approved by the Crown.

Such were the general outlines of the Colonial Governments at the outbreak of the War of the Revolution. Although the Crown claimed great power, the laws were administered in a manner so liberal and humane that the people were contented, and there was on the whole but little complaint, till the effort made by the British Parliament, under George the Third, to tax the colonies. Then came the outbreak of the storm of rebellion and the union of the colonies in a Continental Congress. I need not follow the political history of the period farther than as it bears directly upon my subject. The Congress in the fall of 1775 advised the colonies of New Hampshire, South Carolina and Virginia to form governments adapted to the necessities of the times, and on the 10th of May, 1776, by motion of John Adams, adopted a resolution that "Each one of the United Colonies, where no government sufficient to the exigencies of their affairs had as yet been established, should adopt such government as would, in the opinion of the representatives of the people, best conduce to the happiness and safety of their constituents and of America."

In accordance with the spirit of these resolutions, all the colonies placed their governments on a new basis. Rhode Island simply declared her independence, and continued under the forms of her Charter Government till 1842. Connecticut adopted a brief bill of rights, and continued the old form of government till 1818. The other eleven colonies, in the course of a very few years, adopted new constitutions. Some formed provisional instruments, which were soon replaced by more permanent ones; others rejected the work of their first conventions; but by 1784 the entire eleven had formulated their ideas of republican institutions and adopted them as the basis of government.

The germ of the written constitution is found in the Colonial Charter governments, and the reader will notice that some of the colonies found these early and simple forms sufficient for their needs for many years after their separation from the mother-country. It was four years after the Declaration of Independence before Massachusetts adopted her first State Constitution; while Connecticut continued under her charter forms for 42 years, and Rhode Island 66 years, simply substituting the authority of the people for that of the king.

To the instruments adopted during the War of the Revolution I would call special attention. Crude, ill-digested and ill-balanced as they seem to the historical student of to-day, they are, so far as I know, the first successful efforts to form republican governments upon written constitutions. The conception of an instrument creating the government, and yet restraining it, giving it life and power, and yet limiting and balancing those powers, an instrument which even the people cannot override, except by prescribed forms, this conception was first made a practical success in America and in these constitutions. The British Constitution is an unwritten code of political customs sanctioned by time and protected only by the conservatism of a privileged class and the loyalty of the people. "Parliament," says Cooley, "exercises sovereign authority, and may even change the constitution at any time; but in America the will of the people as declared in the constitution is the final law which governs the legislative body equally with the private citizen." I have said these early constitutions are marked by an undue preponderance of the Legislature, entirely unsettling the balance of the government. As showing how different were the estimates then held of the functions of political machinery from the notions of modern times, I may add that while the simplest constitutional amendment must to-day be submitted to direct popular vote for ratification, most of those early instruments were both framed and adopted by the Legislatures; and where they were framed by special conventions they were, with one or two exceptions, *adopted* finally by the same conventions, and it was not held necessary to submit them to popular vote.

The same confusion prevailed regarding the Confederation of the States which was formed about this same time. That government—if such it could be called, consisting as it did of a Congress solely, having neither executive nor judiciary, —was never submitted to the people of all the States, but was ratified in many of them by the Legislatures alone, a fact commented on by Madison in the *Federalist*, No. 43, in these words: "A compact between independent sovereigns, founded on acts of legislative authority, can pretend to no higher validity than a league or treaty between the parties;" and Edmund Randolph, in his opening speech before the Constitutional Convention at Philadelphia, in 1787, said very truly: "The Confederation was made in the infancy of the science of constitutions."

II.

CONSTITUTIONS OF THE REVOLUTIONARY PERIOD.

In considering the Constitutions of the Revolutionary period, a brief summary of those provisions relating to my subject may be found in Bancroft's United States, Vol. IX., Ch. 15, and in the *Federalist*, No. 46; the full text of the instruments themselves may be found in the two volumes entitled "Charters and Constitutions," published by the United States Government in 1879. No words of mine can give their spirit so well as the pointed language of Madison in the Convention of 1787. He said, "Experience proves a tendency in our governments to throw all power into the Legislative vortex. The Executives of the State are little more than ciphers; the Legislatures are omnipotent. If no effectual check be devised on the encroachments of the latter, a revolution will be inevitable." He might have derived some consolation from the fact that the States which had enjoyed the most liberty as colonies preserved a juster balance of powers in their constitutions, while the latest framed instruments showed a positive improvement on those of earlier date, as if a healthier sentiment had already begun to prevail. But let us examine the documents themselves.

First notice the restrictions of the power of the Executive and his dependence on the Legislature. In nine out of thirteen States the Governor was *chosen* by the Legislature. Only in the four New England States was he elected by the people; and his term was the shortest possible, being in ten States only one year and nowhere over three years. To provide still further against the designs of a cunning Executive, the six Southern States restricted carefully his re-election, providing that he might hold office not more than two or three consecutive years, when he should be ineligible for three or four years. To control his action even more, there was an Executive or Privy Council in every colony whose advice and consent were required to all important acts. This council was usually appointed by the Legislature, and sometimes required to be from its own members.

In eleven States the Governor had no veto whatever on legislation; in Massachusetts he had the usual qualified veto; in New York he, together with the Supreme Court, formed a Council of Revision which wielded a veto power. In the matter of pardoning offenses, in five States the Governor had the pardoning power unrestricted; in four States he could only exercise it with the consent of the Council or Legislature; in Georgia the power belonged to the Legislature alone. The appointing power is one of the chief prerogatives of the Executive. In not one of the States did the Executive wield such a power singly. In Georgia all officers were elected by the people. In three States they were chosen entirely by the Legislature; in four States, mainly by the Legislature; in some, by the Governor and Council; in New York, by the Legislature through an Appointing Committee.

"The Legislature," says Bancroft, "was the center of the

system. The Governor had no power to dissolve it, or either branch. In most of the States all important civil and military officers were elected by the Legislature. The scanty power intrusted to the Governor, wherever his power was more than a shadow, was still further restrained by an Executive Council. Where the Governor had the nomination of officers, they could be commissioned only by consent of the Council." He might have added that the Governor himself was generally elected by the Legislature; that in many States the Legislature could remove any officer; that in some States these bodies held or shared the pardoning power; and, most singular of all, in five States they exercised extensive judicial powers, generally sitting as a Court of last resort.

Warnings of the Revolutionary Statesmen.

And yet the statesmen of that day had a full understanding of the defects. Listen to Madison, in the *Federalist:* "The accumulation of all powers—Legislative, Executive and Judiciary—in the same hands, whether of one, a few, or many, and whether hereditary, self-appointed or elective, may justly be pronounced the very definition of tyranny." After comparing at length the provisions of these State Constitutions, he says: "They carry strong marks of the haste and still stronger of the inexperience under which they were framed, and in some instances the fundamental principle under consideration has been violated by too great a mixture or even an actual consolidation of the different powers."... "The Legislative Department is everywhere extending the sphere of its activity, and drawing all power into its impetuous vortex."... "The founders of our Republic seem never to have recollected the danger from Legislative usurpations, which, by assembling all power in the same hands, must lead to the same tyranny as is threatened by Executive usurpations."... And he quotes from Jefferson's Notes on Virginia the following passage relative to the same defects in the Virginia Constitution: "All the powers of the government—Legislative, Executive and Judiciary—result to the same Legislative body. The concentrating these in the same hands is precisely the definition of despotic government. It will be no alleviation that these powers will be exercised by a plurality of hands, and not by a single one.... An elective despotism was not the government we fought for, but one which should not only be founded on free principles, but in which the powers of the government should be so divided and balanced among several bodies of magistracy as that no one could transcend their legal limits without being effectually checked and restrained by the others."

I cannot better close this part of my subject than by quoting the incisive words of Bancroft, speaking of the spirit which permeated the Articles of Confederation, formed at this very period. "The Confederacy was formed under the influence of political ideas which had been developed by a contest of centuries for individual and local liberties against an irresponsible central authority. Now that power passed to the people, new institutions were required, strong enough to protect the State, while they should leave untouched the liberties of the individual. But America, misled by what belonged to the past, took for her organizing principle, the principle of resistance to power, which in all the thirteen colonies had been hardened into stubbornness by a succession of common jealousies and struggles." Of all the instruments formed at this period, the Massachusetts Constitution of 1780 was by far the best, maintaining the most just balance of power between its departments; and this alone survives, though it has been materially amended. The Federal Constitution, fortunately, was not shaped till 1787, when the evils of these one-sided governments had become evident, and therefore it received more harmonious proportions.

In 105 years, from 1776 to 1880, inclusive, just 105 constitutions, counting in the Articles of Confederation and the

Federal Constitution, had been adopted by the people of these United States, an average of one each year. Of these, 45 belong to the eleven States in rebellion, and this excessive proportion is partly due to their unsettled condition at the close of the civil war. Throwing out these States, the average age of the defunct instruments was about 27 years. There are, however, eight States which have each lived over half a century under one constitution; five New England States under their present forms, Massachusetts 105 years, New Hampshire 93, Vermont 92, Connecticut 67, and Maine 65; Rhode Island from the issuing of her charter to 1842, New Jersey 1776 to 1844, and Kentucky 1799 to 1850. In the above figures I have taken no account of constitutions formulated by conventions and rejected by the people, nor of the innumerable amendments, some very important, which have been adopted or rejected.

Massachusetts bears off the palm for conservatism, living 105 years under one instrument; Kansas for the most frequent changes, having four constitutions in five years, from 1855 to 1859; some of which, however, must be credited to border wars and squatter sovereignty. Eight States are living under their original constitutions. I give them in order of age: Massachusetts 1780, Maine 1820, Rhode Island 1842, Wisconsin 1848, Oregon 1857, Minnesota 1857, Nevada 1864, and Colorado 1876. Four States have each had five successive constitutions: Georgia, South Carolina Texas and Virginia. Louisiana takes the prize for number, having adopted her sixth constitution in 1879. These figures do not include any changes that may have taken place during the rebellion, under the Confederacy, from 1861 to 1865.

Under the early revolutionary constitutions, the Legislature soon began to invade the other powers of the government. Madison said, in 1787: "The tendency of republican governments is to aggrandize the Legislature at the expense of the other departments." The nearer the people, the greater the audacity of aggression. This tendency was noticed very early; its progress is marked in the *Federalist*, No. 47, as it manifested itself in New York and Pennsylvania. Soon a desire for its correction began to be seen; first conspicuously in the New York Constitution of 1846. This modern spirit shows itself by separating the functions of the three departments and making each independent, so far as it can be done; it is distinguished everywhere by a restriction of the Legislature, an increase of Executive power and by independence of both Governor and Judges. I cannot consider each of these instruments in detail, but will only point out their general features; and I should add that this review includes the Louisiana Constitution of 1868, but not that of 1879, of which I had no details.

III.

MODERN STATE CONSTITUTIONS.

To-day the Governor is everywhere chosen by the people directly, instead of through the Legislature; his term has generally been much lengthened, the old term of one year being retained in only four New England States, while in fifteen States it has been lengthened to two years, in two States to three years, and in seventeen States, including nearly all with late constitutions, to four years. At the same time, the old restrictions on consecutive terms and re-election have been generally abrogated, being retained in only eight States to-day. The veto power has been restored, and at present in thirty-four States the Governor has the usual qualified veto on legislation. In nine of these, however, the veto may be overruled by a bare majority of each house of the Legislature. Four States—Delaware, North Carolina, Ohio and Rhode Island—have absolutely no veto. As the Legislature is apt to crowd much business into the last days of its sessions, twenty States, to prevent crude and hasty legislation, allow the Governor some time after the adjournment to consider whether he will sign or veto a bill, and thirteen States permit him to veto individual items in an appropriation bill; of this I will speak presently more at length. The Privy Council has been abolished in all but three States, and in these it is no longer chosen by the Legislature, but by the people, and its control over the Governor is much curtailed.

The appointing of officers has been generally taken from the Legislature. Most of the officers are chosen by the people; where this is not the case, they are usually appointed by the Governor and confirmed by the Council or the upper house of the Legislature. The pardoning power is now everywhere vested in the Governor, or the Governor acting with the advice of either the Council or the Courts—except in Connecticut, where the Legislature retains the power. In most of the States the Legislature is forbidden to increase or decrease the salary of the Governor during the period for which he was elected. Such are the leading points in which the power and independence of the Executive Department have been restored. The Judiciary has also been placed upon a new footing. The Legislatures have been stripped of their judicial functions, except in cases of impeachment, and the Judges, instead of being elected by the Legislatures, are now, with the exception of four States, chosen by the people, or appointed by the Governor and confirmed by the Council or Senate. The relations of the Judiciary to the other great departments of government will be more fully treated hereafter.

Limitations upon Legislation.

Not satisfied with this transfer of powers to the other branches of the government, a general desire has grown up to curtail legislation, and a new system of checks upon law-making has been devised, giving rise to such provisions as the following: Biennial sessions of the Legislatures have been substituted for annual meetings in twenty-five constitutions, including all the later ones. The length of the sessions has been shortened in half of the States, sometimes by prescribing an absolute limit, sometimes by curtailing the pay of members after a certain time, running in different States from 40 to 90 days; and experience shows that their zeal to serve their country as legislators dies out with their pay. Special legislation is forbidden by stringent provisions in many States. In special sessions, the Legislatures of many States are forbidden to consider subjects not mentioned in the call for the session, and special sessions are in ten constitutions limited in length, varying from fifteen to forty days.

To prevent hasty legislation, some States forbid the introduction of any new bill (unless, perhaps, by a two-thirds vote of each house) after a certain period has elapsed from the beginning of the session, which period ranges in different places from 25 to 6c days. In other cases, new bills cannot be introduced within a certain number of days of the period set for the adjournment. Some constitutions provide that all bills and amendments must be printed and published before they can be considered by either house. All must be read three times in each house, usually on different days. In nineteen States no bill can be passed except by a majority of the members elected to each house, and the yeas and nays must be recorded on the final passage of every bill. Twenty-three States provide that no Act shall be revised or amended by mere reference to its title, but the Act revised or section amended shall be set forth and published at full length. And, as already stated, where the Governor holds the veto power he may usually have a certain number of days to consider the bill, even if the Legislature should adjourn in the meantime.

Perhaps the most fruitful source of vicious legislation is found in "log-rolling,"—that is, combining two or more subjects in one bill,—or in "riders" upon appropriation bills,—that is, in grafting general or special legislation upon some bill containing the general appropriations for the support of the government,—or in combining appropriations for special purposes with the general appropriations,—or in hurrying through some vicious measure under a specious or false title. All these, except the last, are direct assaults upon the independence of the Executive, compelling him to give his assent to objectionable measures, or, in vetoing them, to veto measures of public necessity. The question of "riders" upon appropriation bills will be more fully considered in connection with the Federal Government. To prevent these evils has been the object of many constitutional provisions, and the practice has been broken up in most of the States by clauses providing that no bill shall contain more than one subject, which shall be clearly expressed by the title, or forbidding the insertion of private appropriations in the general appropriation bills; while in fourteen States, as already remarked, the Governor has power to veto any single item in an appropriation bill.

Besides all the checks on unwholesome legislation which I have mentioned, there are many others much in vogue with modern constitution-makers, such as the following: It is quite customary to forbid the incurring of any indebtedness by the State; to forbid any loan of its credit; to forbid any increase or diminution of the pay of members of the Legislature during their term of office (the same provision is common regarding other officers of the State); no money shall be drawn from the treasury except by appropriation bills; legislators shall not be appointed to any office created by them; the order of the payment of the appropriations is often prescribed; no continuing appropriation shall be made for over two years; no extra compensation shall be allowed to officers during their term of office; no term of office of any individual shall be extended; no legislator shall be interested in any contract with the State; no person holding any lucrative office under the State or United States shall sit in the Legislature; no bill shall be amended so as to change its purpose; no money shall be given from the State treasury to any institution of a sectarian character; no special privileges shall be granted to any corporation; and lastly, the Judges of the

Supreme Court are sometimes associated with the upper house in the trial of impeachments. All these provisions, and other similar ones much in use, are checks upon the power of the Legislature, and would have been thought strange and unnatural restrictions a hundred years ago. Indeed, this desire to control and limit the government is shown throughout the general character of these new constitutions. It extends in some respects, though in a limited degree, to the powers of the Executive and Judiciary, and it forms a striking contrast to the generous confidence which the people placed in their officers a century ago, and the liberal powers entrusted to them. The early instruments were usually very short, being often simply a bill of rights, followed by a mere skeleton of the government. Those of to-day are lengthy than a fundamental instrument. The officers of the State are documents, full of detail, frequently more like a code of laws limited and cramped in their action in every direction. Two of the most remarkable for their length are the constitutions adopted by Maryland in 1867, and by California in 1879.

The Southern Confederacy.

The Constitution framed by the Southern Confederacy in 1861 gives a curious evidence of this change in the ideas of our people regarding the relations of the Executive and Legislative branches of government. It follows very closely the Constitution of the United States, but with the following differences, among others: The heads of the departments have seats on the floor of each House of Congress. The President may veto items in an appropriation bill. Congress shall appropriate no money except by a two-thirds vote of both houses, taken by yeas and nays, unless the appropriation is asked for by the head of some department of the government, or is to pay its own expenses or some judicial award against the government. No bill shall comprise more than one subject, and that shall be fully expressed in its title. The term of office of the Executive shall be six years, and he shall not be re-eligible. The heads of departments may be removed by the President; other officers are removable only for good cause, to be expressed in a report to Congress.

Thus we see that in the State Constitutions there has been a steady drift of popular opinion towards limiting the powers of the Legislature, and, as a rule, towards increasing those of the Executive. This has arisen partly from the need of a better balance between the departments, and partly from a wish to check crude and unwholesome legislation. It is observable that on the whole this drift is strongest in the newer communities, while the older States, especially those whose people are better educated, and where a more active public spirit prevails, have made fewer changes.

IV.

THE FEDERAL GOVERNMENT.

Without further discussing the State Governments let us pass at once to the Federal Constitution. Nothing can be more instructive than to pause a moment at the threshold and trace some of the hesitating steps by which the fathers reached this admirable form of government, and in the beginning let me acknowledge my debt to Bancroft's History of the Constitution, which has been my sure guide. The Confederation, that "rope of sand," was rapidly crumbling away. It was at best a Congress only, without Executive or Judiciary, hardly more than a league of independent States against Great Britain. Its feeble vitality ended when the pressure of war was removed. The memory of the galling exactions of King and Parliament had made the States afraid to trust even the servants of their own choosing, and the impotent Congress became the laughing-stock of the nations of Europe. "America," in the words of her great historian, "carried with her in her progress the urn which held the ashes of the dead past, but she had also hope and creative power."

The wise men of the day met at Philadelphia in 1787, to devise a plan for a more stable government. We can consider only those features of the convention which related to the balance of powers within the proposed government. The question met them on the threshold, how should the Executive be chosen and of how many should it consist? Virginia proposed that it should be chosen by Congress, leaving the number undetermined. New Jersey preferred a plural Executive, to be chosen and removable by Congress. Williamson of North Carolina proposed a triple Executive, to be chosen from the Northern, Middle and Southern States. Hamilton wanted a single President, chosen by electors, to hold during good behavior; others preferred a direct choice by the people. At last, after weary discussions, the convention voted—seven States to three—that the Executive power should be in one man, and afterwards determined that he should be chosen by Congress. A little later they reconsidered the mode of election, and declared in favor of an electoral system something like the present one; then they placed the choice again in the hands of Congress, and at last they settled down as a finality upon the present system. See how narrowly we escaped having the President chosen by Congress; and yet Madison said in the convention it was so essential to keep the three departments independent of each other, he thought "a tenure of good behavior for the Executive a less evil than its dependence on the National Legislature for re-election," and others spoke in the same vein.

A strong effort was made to engraft on the Constitution a Privy Council, which should be chosen by Congress and should share to some extent the duties and responsibilities of the Executive, especially relating to the confirmation of appointments and ratification of treaties. This effort to limit the power of the President failed to pass the convention, and its failure compelled the substitution of the Senate in the performance of some of its functions; thus at the last moment the convention invested the Senate with the power to confirm appointments and ratify treaties made by the Executive. "Wilson of Pennsylvania was most apprehensive that the Legislature, by swallowing up all the other powers, would lead to a dissolution of the government; no adequate self-defensive power having been granted either to the Executive or Judicial departments." He foreshadowed the power of the Senate in these prophetic words: "The President will not be the man of the people, but the minion of the Senate. He cannot even appoint a tide-waiter without it." Wilson's fear was well founded, so far as the appointments were concerned; but it certainly would not have been prudent to leave this tremendous power uncontrolled in the hands of one man.

THE OPPOSITION TO A STRONG JUDICIARY.

This sketch of the sentiments of the convention regarding the relative powers to be entrusted to the various departments would not be complete without a brief notice of their action concerning the Judiciary. A strong opposition was manifested to entrusting the Federal Judiciary with those ample powers necessary for a stable government. It came from two sources. The Confederation had had no Judiciary; and the friends of the State governments were very unwilling to give the Federal Courts power to declare a State statute in conflict with the Federal Constitution; while the advocates of legislative power maintained that it was dangerous to allow the Judges to override a statute enacted by Congress. It was said by Mercer, of Maryland: "I disapprove the doctrine that the Judges, as expositors of the Constitution, have authority to declare a law void. Laws ought to be well and cautiously made, and then be uncontrollable." This would have been virtually giving Congress the sovereign control possessed by the English Parliament, and illustrates well how little some of these men yet understood the full meaning of the new American doctrine of an instrument controlling and limiting the very government established under it. Fortunately there were wiser men, who thought with Hamilton: "The Courts of Justice should be the bulwarks of a limited constitution against legislative encroachments." The good sense of the Convention brushed aside these jealousies and gave the Judiciary the ample powers it now possesses. Of the growth of these powers by judicial construction I will speak presently. Another influence, supported by such men as Madison, Wilson and Morris, would have combined the Judges of the Supreme Court with the President in the exercise of the veto power, after the model of the Council of Revision in New York, unmindful of the danger of mingling the powers of the different departments. This, too, was happily overruled in the convention.

I have sketched these discussions in the convention to show the difficulties that surrounded the framers of the Constitution, even on points that seem to us perfectly clear. But the wisdom drawn from ten years' experience with the Revolutionary State Constitutions and the Confederation, shed a flood of light on their work. The structure they raised, that model of balanced powers, has outlived a century of political convulsions, and yet stands alone in its just proportions and harmonious outline. "As the British Constitution," said Gladstone, "is the most subtile organism which has proceeded from progressive history, so the American Constitution is the most wonderful work ever struck off at a given time by the brain and purpose of man." Be it remembered to the honor of the Southern States, that they were a majority in the convention.

Balance of Powers in Federal Government.

Notice the care with which the powers of the different branches are balanced and guarded in this wonderful instrument. First, the power of Congress is limited, by its division into two houses. Of this division Judge Story says: "It is of vital importance to interpose some check against the undue exercise of the legislative power, which in every government is the predominating and almost irresistible power.... A second branch of the Legislative Assembly doubles the security to the people by requiring the concurrence of two distinct bodies in schemes of usurpation and perfidy." This principle is carried into the impeachment of the Executive; after the model of the British Parliament, he must be impeached by the lower, but tried by the upper house. Improper legislation on the part of Congress can be checked by the veto of the Executive, but this again can be overruled by two-thirds of each house; of which Judge Story remarks: "There is a natural tendency in the Legislative Department to intrude upon the rights and absorb the powers of the other departments of government. A mere parchment delineation of the boundaries of each is wholly insufficient for the protection of the weaker branch, as the Executive unquestionably is, and hence there arises a constitutional necessity of arming it with powers for its own defense. If the Executive did not possess this qualified negative he would be gradually stripped of all his authority, and become what it is well known the Governors of some States are, a mere pageant and shadow of magistracy."

Another provision to secure the independence of the Executive is that forbidding an increase or diminution of the President's salary during the term for which he is elected; while the Judges of the Supreme Court are protected by a similar provision forbidding the diminution of their salaries. In case of removal, death, resignation or inability of the President, a Vice-President chosen by the people assumes the Executive power, and not until a similar disaster befalls the Vice-President has Congress any power to designate a successor. No Senator or Representative shall be appointed a Presidential Elector. No person holding any office under the United States shall be a member of either house during his continuance in office. Under this clause no member of either house can be a Cabinet officer while holding his seat in Congress. On the other hand the rights of Congress are as carefully guarded from invasion by the Executive. The control of the public purse is confined exclusively to them. "No money shall be drawn from the Treasury but in consequence of appropriations made by law."

The President has no power to dissolve or adjourn Congress, except in case of disagreement between the two Houses. Under the Colonial Governments it had been held a great grievance, so great as to be mentioned in the Declaration of Independence, that the King had repeatedly dissolved the Colonial Legislatures and refused to re-assemble them, thus depriving the people of representation. The Constitution provides that "the Congress shall assemble at least once every year, and such meeting shall be on the first Monday in December, unless they shall by law appoint a different day." The value to Congress of this independence was shown during Johnson's administration, when Congress, being at war with the President, remained continuously in session for two years, with occasional recesses of one to four months. The appointing of all leading officers is vested in the President, with the consent of the Senate. The appointment of inferior officers may by law be vested in the President, the Courts of Law, or the heads of the Departments. The confirmation of the leading officers by the Senate is the only power Congress has over appointments.

Such great care was taken to separate the functions of the President and Congress. But though the Executive was intrenched behind much stronger powers than those granted by the early State Constitutions, it has been unable to prevent some encroachments by the Legislature upon its functions. In the above enumeration I have not mentioned the awkward provision for the election of a President by the House voting by States, where no candidate has a majority of the

Electors, because it only provides for a rare emergency, and is not likely to exercise any permanent influence on the relations of the two departments; moreover the House can only choose from the three highest candidates already voted for by the Electors. The authority assumed of late years by Congress to canvass the Electoral vote is a far more dangerous power.

Encroachments of Congress.

Smyth, in his Lectures on Modern History, written in 1811, from an English standpoint, says: "If there results to America a grand calamity and failure of the whole, it can only accrue from the friends of liberty not venturing to render the Executive power sufficiently effective—the common mistake of all popular governments." Wherever the limits of the President's power and that of Congress overlapped one another, Congress has usually tried to occupy the debatable ground. I shall notice but three points of conflict; first, the treaty-making power; second, coercive legislation, or, to use the ordinary term, "political riders" on appropriation bills, and third, the power of appointing and removing officers.

The treaty-making power is vested by the Constitution in the President and the Senate, in these terms, "He (the President) shall have power, by and with the advice and consent of the Senate, to make treaties, provided two-thirds of the Senators present concur." In the face of this provision, Congress has assumed the power by the form of an ordinary statute to abrogate treaties, as was done in 1798, when our treaty relations with France were terminated by statute, and to abrogate portions of treaties so far as they relate to internal domestic matters. This action was sustained by Judge Curtis, in *Taylor* v. *Morton*, 2 Curtis, 454, which established this point, that an Act of Congress may supersede a prior treaty, so far as it is a municipal law, provided the subject matter is within the legislative power of Congress. This position has been repeatedly sustained by the Courts. But further, the House of Representatives claims the right to pass upon all treaties affecting the revenue, by virtue of that clause in the Constitution giving the House the right to originate all bills for raising revenue. In acknowledgment of this claim the terms of the Hawaiian Reciprocity Treaty provided that it should not go into effect until the passage of an Act by Congress to carry it into effect. The Act was passed and approved August 15, 1876, and the convention proclaimed September 9.

Political Riders.

The expedient of "tacking," as it is called in England—that is, of legislating on appropriation bills—first appeared in the American Congress about 1846. Nine years later, in 1855, it was first tried as a means of compelling legislation. There was a difference between the Senate and the House on the tariff question; the house put a tariff clause on the Civil and Diplomatic Appropriation bill. The Senate promptly protested against it as improper legislation and rejected it, in which the House concurred, and the bill was passed without the rider. In 1856 a similar attempt was made and met the same fate. So far, it will be observed, the "political rider" only appeared as a weapon in a contest between the two Houses of Congress. From 1865 to 1869 took place the great struggle between Congress and President Johnson. During this, in 1867, the famous bill, virtually depriving the President of the command of the army and placing its management in the hands of General Grant, was passed as a rider upon the Army Appropriation bill. Johnson protested, but signed the bill; a veto would have been useless, as his opponents had over two-thirds of both houses and would have passed the bill over his veto. From this time forward the practice of legislating on appropriation bills became more and more common, mainly as a matter of convenience. The number of bills introduced into Congress is so large, sometimes reaching 8000 or 10,000, that it is almost impossible to obtain a hearing for any measure. But the appropriation bills *must* be passed, and it has become very common to place on them provisions enacting necessary laws which otherwise could not be reached on the calendar. Judge Reagan, of Texas, said, in the House of Representatives, that between 1862 and 1875, 387 measures of general legislation had been passed as provisos upon appropriation bills. Ten years ago the practice had become so objectionable that General Grant, in his Message, December 1, 1873, advised an amendment of the Constitution which would prevent it, and this recommendation was recently renewed by President Arthur, in his Message of December 5, 1882. The House of Representatives also recognized the faulty nature of the practice, and amended its rules so as to forbid legislation on appropriation bills, except when it is germane to the subject of the bill and in the interest of economy.

President Hayes and Congress.

The practice continued, however, in a modified form, and when in the 46th Congress the dominant party in both houses wanted to compel the assent of President Hayes to certain political legislation, they had recourse to this expedient and tacked the obnoxious measures upon the bills appropriating money for the support of the army and for the payment of United States Marshals. A struggle ensued between the two parties in Congress, lasting three months, which will be famous in history as defining one of the great landmarks of the government. The bills at last passed both Houses with the riders, and were vetoed by President Hayes. After seven successive vetoes, five of which were upon appropriation bills with riders attached, and two upon the riders detached from the appropriations, the two Houses gave up the struggle and passed the bills without the riders.

The veto message of April 30, 1879, on the Army Bill, discusses the question at length. I quote a few passages from it: "The practice of tacking to appropriation bills measures not pertinent to such bills, did not prevail until more than forty years after the adoption of the Constitution. It has become a common practice. All parties when in power have adopted it. Many abuses and great waste of public money have in this way crept into appropriation bills. The public opinion of the country is against it. The States which have recently adopted constitutions have generally provided a remedy for the evil by enacting that no law shall contain more than one subject, which shall be plainly expressed in its title. The constitutions of more than half the States contain substantially this provision.".... "The principle (maintained by Congress) is that the House of Representatives has the sole right to originate bills for raising revenue, and therefore has the right to withhold appropriations upon which the existence of the government may depend, unless the Senate and the President shall give their assent to any legislation which the House may see fit to attach to appropriation bills. To establish this principle is to make a radical, dangerous and unconstitutional change in the character of our institutions.".... "The new doctrine, if maintained, will result in a consolidation of unchecked and despotic power in the House of Representatives. A bare majority of the House will become the government. The Executive will no longer be what the framers of the Constitution intended, an equal and independent branch of the Government.".... "The House alone will be the judge of what constitutes a grievance and also of the means and measure of redress.".... "Believing this bill is a dangerous violation of the spirit and meaning of the Constitution, I am compelled to return it to the House in which it originated without my approval."

There was a vast difference between the position of President Hayes and that of President Johnson. In 1867 the dominant party in Congress had the requisite strength to pass the bill over a veto; while in 1879 they had only a bare majority in each House, and could only control the Executive, to refuse the supplies necessary for the maintenance of the Government, or, as it was tersely put by General Garfield, they threatened to "starve the Government," unless their demands were complied with. It was an entirely new line of attack upon the Executive, and having met with absolute defeat, it is not likely to be renewed by either political party in our day.

Appointment and Removal of Officers.

But the most direct assault on the power of the President is the Senate's encroachment on his power of appointment and removal. The terms of the appointing power are distinctly stated in the Constitution, but nothing is said of removals. The question came up in 1789, under Washington's administration, whether Cabinet officers appointed by the President with the consent of the Senate could be removed by the President alone, or whether their removal should require the consent of the Senate. Congress, influenced perhaps by the exalted character of Washington, passed the bill allowing the President the power of removal in these cases. This action was opposed by many of the wisest men of that day; a powerful minority resisted it in the House, and it passed the Senate only by the casting vote of the Vice-President. Of course it carried with it the acknowledgment of the principle that the power of removing officers lay in the Executive, though I do not suppose that any man then imagined the terrible abuse which would, inside of half a century, follow the use of that power. The action of Congress in this matter is spoken of by Story as "the most extraordinary case in the history of the government, of a power conferred by implication on the Executive by the assent of a bare majority of Congress, which has not been questioned on many other occasions." Very soon, however, after the publication of this opinion, this "legislative construction," as it was called, of a constitutional provision, became the subject of a very spirited debate in Congress during Jackson's first term of office. Story's Commentaries on the Constitution contain an interesting discussion of the original debate in Congress in 1789, while a careful review of the President's side of the question may be found in Johnson's Message, March 2, 1867, vetoing the Tenure of Office Act.

To the Victors Belong the Spoils.

No marked result followed from this policy adopted in 1789, till Jackson became President in 1829, when, as is well known, a general removal of civil officers took place for the first time. This created a great outcry and much bitter feeling. A very able debate on the President's course took place in the Senate, in which the Whigs censured him for exceeding his rightful powers; no further action, however, ensued, as the House of Representatives was friendly to Jackson. But from this time forward a change came over the policy of the Government in these matters. "To the victors belong the spoils," was recognized as the governing motive of each party when in power. Each President in turn, on taking his seat, removed his enemies from public office and appointed his friends. At last there came a time in 1867, when the opposition to the President was strong enough in Congress to control his policy and override his vetoes, for the first time in the history of the country; and under Johnson, the Tenure of Office Act was passed, which reversed the precedent, and forbade the displacement of an officer appointed with the consent of the Senate, unless removed by a similar formality. President Johnson vetoed the bill, but it was passed over his head, and, in a modified form, it is the law to-day. On the accession of General Grant to the Presidency the law was amended, but the Senate have never parted with the power. Thus the power of removal, without the consent of the Senate, was taken from the Executive.

But great as this loss was to the President, he has sustained a still greater one in the virtual deprival of the power of appointment. Already in the days of Jackson, the party leaders in the Senate began to claim the appointment of their supporters to public office, and this practice was steadily gaining ground with each Administration. The contest with President Johnson expanded the power and the ambition of the Senate still more, and the Senators now demanded, as the price of their support of the Administration, that the more important Federal appointments in their respective States should be made from their adherents. The Executive was obliged to yield—even Grant could not resist—and so the modern "boss" was established. To-day the Senatorial "boss" controls the large majority of Presidential appointments, in unquestionable violation of the intent of the Constitution.

There is a curious trifle in the matter of social etiquette at Washington, which marks the rising tide of Senatorial dignity at the time we have been speaking of. In Washington society, as is well known, social precedence follows strictly the order of political rank; before Johnson's time the Cabinet officers outranked the Senators; but, under Grant, the Senatorial dignity claimed a place at the dinner table above the Secretary, and the claim was recognized. This seems laughable, but the demand was backed by real power.

This vicious and unconstitutional practice of dictating Executive appointments has grown until now the "courtesy of the Senate," so called, that is, the tacit agreement with each other to divide the spoils, often overrides all considerations of individual fitness or of public interest. The climax was reached when two United States Senators resigned their seats because they could not have their share of the patronage. The world moves on and there is a high-water-mark for every iniquity. The Dred Scott case marked the full swell of the tide of the power of slavery; the veto of the Army bill in 1879 sounded the decline of "political riders." The resignation of the New York Senators was the dawn of a new era without "bosses." It brings the hope of something better than a restoration of the power of removal to the Executive. We want no more Jacksons; the concentration of all this power in one man would be more dangerous than in a Senate of 76 members; but we look forward for that better time when there shall be no appointments except for fitness, and no removal but for just cause.

Jackson's Extraordinary Claims.

In reviewing the political history of the country, we find that while Congress and the Executive have often been at variance, they have three times openly joined battle on the extent of their prerogatives. The first fight was between Jackson and the Whigs in 1834, the second between Johnson and the Republicans in 1867, and the third between Hayes and the Democrats in 1879. I have already referred to Jackson's wholesale decapitation of the Federal officials, upon his accession to the Presidency, and the indignation expressed by his opponents at this new departure in political warfare. Towards the end of his first term he became involved in a war with the United States Bank, and vetoed the bill extending its charter, alleging, among other objections, that the charter was unconstitutional, although the Supreme Court had sustained the original Act. In his veto message occurs this remarkable passage: "If the opinion of the Supreme Court covered the whole ground of this Act, it ought not to control the coordinate authorities of this Government. The Congress, the Executive, and the Court, must, each for itself, be guided by its own opinion of the Constitution. Each public officer who takes an oath to support the Constitution, swears that he will support it as he understands it, and not as it is understood by others. It is as much the duty of the House of Representatives, of the Senate, and of the President, to decide upon the constitutionality of any bill or resolution which may be presented to them for passage or approval, as it is of the Supreme Judges, when it may be brought before them for judicial decision. The opinion of the Judges has no more authority over Congress than the opinion of Congress has over the Judges, and on that point the President is independent of both. The authority of the Supreme Court must not, therefore, be permitted to control Congress or the Executive, when acting in their legislative capacities, but to have only such influence as the force of their reasoning may deserve."

Jackson was an exceedingly positive, self-willed, arbitrary man, of remarkable tenacity of purpose. He was dear to the people as the hero of New Orleans, and was universally respected as a man of sturdy honesty, integrity of purpose and inflexible patriotism. His fight with the bank increased his popularity, for it made him the champion of the poor as against the rich, of the laboring classes as against the moneyed interests, and shortly after the veto he was re-elected President. Jackson's re-election should not be regarded as a verdict by the people in favor of the spoils system, or of his despotic assumption of power, but as an expression of their love for him as a soldier, and their prejudice against what they conceived to be the moneyed rule as represented by the Whigs. Emboldened by his re-election, he determined to remove the Government deposits from the United States Bank, although Congress had declared in favor of their retention there. Duane, the Secretary of the Treasury, refused to do it. Jackson removed him and appointed Taney, afterwards Chief Justice of the Supreme Court, as his successor, and Taney removed the deposits in September, 1833. When the new Congress met in December, the House was favorable to Jackson, but the Senate resolved, March 28, 1834, that "the President, in the late proceedings in relation to the public revenue, has assumed upon himself authority and power not conferred by the Constitution and laws, but in derogation of both."

Jackson replied by the famous "Protest," which he demanded should be entered on the journal of the Senate. He justified his removal of the Secretary of the Treasury by the bold claim that "the power of removal, which, like that of appointment, is an original executive power, is left unchecked by the Constitution, in relation to all Executive officers for whose conduct the President is responsible;" as though, instead of his being invested only with granted powers, there were original Executive powers, part of which only had been removed by the Constitution, while the rest remained. In another part of the Protest, he declared "the President is the direct representative of the American people, elected by the people and responsible to them," while "the Senate is a body not directly amenable to the people," thus assuming a kind of patriarchal duty to stand between the Senate and the people. The Senate passed a second series of resolutions, to the effect that the Protest "ascribed powers to the President irreconcilable with the authority of the two Houses of Congress and with the Constitution," and they refused to enter the Protest on their journal, and here the matter ended for a while. The House being friendly to Jackson, the Senate could do no more. In the next Congress, however, Jackson's friends controlled the Senate and expunged the obnoxious resolution of March 28, 1834, from the Senate journal. When I was a child, the memory of this expunging resolution was fresh, and I well remember the indignation of the Whigs at what they called a mutilation of the records. The student of political history will find a masterly statement of the position of Jackson's opponents in Webster's speeches on the Veto of the Bank Bill, the Removal of the Deposits, the President's Protest and the Expunging Resolution. No President after Jackson ever dared to take the stand he had occupied as to the relative functions of Congress and the President.

His claim of original Executive power, his assumption of a peculiarly close relation to the people empowering him to stand between them and the Senate as the champion of popular rights, and his declaration of his right to be the judge of the constitutionality of laws, would, if allowed, have made him little less than dictator. Von Holst quotes Story as saying of Jackson: "I confess that I feel humiliated at the truth, which cannot be disguised, that though we live under the form of a republic we are in fact under the rule of a single man." Jackson's unbounded popularity sustained him in these arbitrary measures. The people admired him for his military glory, the masses looked up to him as their champion against the rich, all patriots respected him for the stand he took against nullification, while even his enemies gave him the credit of positive convictions and fearlessness in carrying them out. Fortunately for the country he had no successor able to wear his mantle. Congress resumed its accustomed functions, and throughout the Presidency of Van Buren was in fairly harmonious relations with the Executive.

But in Tyler's administration the President was once more in open conflict with both Houses of Congrèss, a conflict embittered by the fact that he had been elected Vice-President by the dominant party. Twice he vetoed the bill re-establishing the United States Bank, and twice he vetoed the Tariff Bill, on which had been tacked a bill for the distribution of the proceeds of the public lands. By this time the indignation of the Whigs was thoroughly aroused; the committee of the House, to which the veto had been referred, with John Quincy Adams at its head, denounced this wholesale exercise of the veto power as tyrannical, and declared they would impeach the President, were there any prospect of his conviction; and Henry Clay introduced a proposition to amend the Constitution so that a majority vote in both Houses of Congress would override a veto. This proposition received a majority of the votes of the House, but not the necessary two-thirds. The President replied to these violent attacks by a Protest, much in the spirit of Jackson's; and here the matter ended, as the Whigs had only a bare majority in each House, and could follow it no farther.

Congress and Andrew Johnson.

There was no open breach after this between the President and Congress till 1866 and 1867. Johnson, who was as positive as General Jackson, but without his support, either in Congress or by the people, had resolved upon a plan of restoring the rebellious States to the Union. The Republican leaders disapproved of the President's measures, and having control of both Houses, by over two-thirds of each, they resolved upon a policy of their own. In pursuance of this policy Congress passed the following four bills, of vital importance in the matter of reconstruction: The Civil Rights Bill, conferring Federal citizenship on all persons born in the United States, and ensuring them full and equal benefit of all laws; the Reconstruction Bill, reversing the President's policy and defining the terms and methods under which the States lately in rebellion could resume their places in the Government; the Civil Tenure Act, stripping him of the power of removing civil officers without the consent of the Senate; and the Electoral College Bill, defining what votes should be counted for President. All these Johnson promptly vetoed and they were immediately passed over his veto. Congress also added to the Army Appropriation Bill a provision which virtually deprived him of the use of the army in aid of his policy of reconstruction, and disbanded the militia of the rebellious States. The President protested against this provision, but signed the bill. Thus Congress rejected the President's plan for the restoration of the Southern States to the Union, and adopted one of their own, while at the same time they stripped him of the power to thwart their policy.

The contest ended in the impeachment of the President, which failed of success by a vote of 35 to 19: one vote more would have deprived him of his seat. It is the most dramatic scene in the history of our country, this mighty struggle for mastery between these two grand powers of the Government. I am not concerned here with the right or the policy of these measures, but simply rehearse them to show the tremendous power of Congress, and the feebleness of the Excutive making war upon it. Congress has absolute control of the Treasury, and when the dominant party numbers two-thirds of each House it holds the absolute power of legislation, within the Constitution, and the power of impeachment. Johnson appealed to Jackson's policy, but was powerless to follow his example.

The third battle, that between Hayes and the Democrats, has been related in sufficient detail already. Thus I have sketched the leading features of encroachment, whether by President or Congress upon its co-ordinate power, since 1789. Jackson's protest in 1834 was the climax of Presidential claims. Johnson's impeachment marks the summit of self-assertion by Congress. Since the accession of Grant, the political pendulum has been slowly swinging towards a limitation of the relative power of Congress. Hayes' victory over the political riders, and the steadfast refusal of both Hayes and Garfield to listen to the dictation of Senatorial leaders, are marked features of the last six years. Two bills recently before Congress emphasize this tendency. One, which has become the law of the land, is the Civil Service Reform Bill, which is really a bill to limit the patronage of Senators; the other is the proposition to change the order of succession, substituting after the Vice-President, the members of the Cabinet, in place of the President of the Senate and the Speaker of the House.

The Veto Power.

The use of the veto power demands a brief notice here, for an impression prevails that it is becoming more common in these latter days. This is not true relatively, when we consider the enormous increase of legislation by Congress. I have been at considerable pains to gather, not only all the vetoes, but as far as possible all the bills retained by the

Presidents, after the adjournment of Congress, or, to use the common phrase, "pocketed." My list may not be absolutely complete, but is very nearly so. I find from Washington to Arthur, inclusive, seventy-seven vetoes of both kinds. Forty-three of these emanated from four Presidents, viz.: Jackson, eleven; Tyler, ten; Johnson, thirteen; Hayes, nine. All these administrations were periods of fierce conflict with a hostile Congress. Add Madison, six; Pierce, five; Buchanan, seven, and Grant, six, and we have sixty-seven out of seventy-seven vetoes; and only ten remain to the other twelve Presidents, covering ten full and four fractional terms.

Dividing the administrations into four consecutive periods, we have this result: From Washington to John Quincy Adams inclusive, a period of forty years, there were nine vetoes; from Jackson to Tyler, in sixteen years, there were twenty-one vetoes; from Polk to Lincoln, twenty years, eight vetoes; from Johnson to Hayes, again sixteen years, twenty-eight vetoes. Five subjects comprise the majority of all the vetoes: Internal Improvements, seventeen; United States Bank, four; Reconstruction Acts, seven; Rebel Claims, four; Interference at Elections by marshals and soldiers, seven, in all thirty-nine out of seventy-seven. Ten bills have been passed over vetoes, one under Tyler, seven under Johnson, one under Hayes, and one under Arthur.

Fierce attacks have been made from time to time in Congress upon the veto power, charging the Presidents with despotic use of it, and claiming that the intention of the founders of the Government was to limit its use to hasty or unconstitutional legislation; but the Constitution itself makes no such limitation, nor does the early practice under it; the second veto of Washington being based solely on expediency and the maintenance of the public faith. The veto power may be dangerous, as all power is in the hands of bad men, but this review does not justify the common impression of its growing abuse. It comes into prominence when the President is brought face to face with a hostile Congress, eager to cross swords with him, but when the two great powers are on friendly terms, as is usually the case, the knowledge of its hidden power acts only as a check upon crude legislation.

Our examination has thus far shown that the disposition of legislatures is aggressive. Every popular body tries to overstep the bounds of its lawful power, from the American Congress down to the County Committee. The Revolutionary fathers, recoiling from the tyranny of royal Governors, gave too much scope to legislative authority. We have been steadily hemming in that authority in our State Constitutions for a century, and expanding the powers of our Governors.

The Federal Constitution, fortunately framed later, in the light of ten years' experience, was much better balanced. But a different principle comes in here. Cooley thus defines the distinction: "It is to be borne in mind that there is a broad distinction between the Constitution of the United States and the Constitutions of the States, as regards the powers which may be exercised under them. The Government of the United States is one of enumerated powers; the Governments of the States are possessed of all the general powers of legislation. When a law of Congress is assailed as void, we look in the National Constitution to see if the grant of specified powers is broad enough to embrace it; but when a State law is attacked on the same ground, it is presumably valid in any case, and this presumption is a conclusive one, unless in the Constitution of the United States or of the State we are able to discover that it is prohibited. We look in the Constitution of the United States for grants of legislative power, but in the Constitution of the State to ascertain if any limitations have been imposed upon the complete power with which the legislative department of the State was vested in its creation. Congress can pass no laws but such as the Constitution authorizes, either expressly or by clear implication; while the State Legislature has jurisdiction of all subjects on which its legislation is not prohibited. 'The law-making power of the State,' it is said in one case, 'recognizes no restraints and is bound by none, except such as are imposed by the Constitution. That instrument has been aptly termed a legislative act by the people themselves in their sovereign capacity, and is therefore the paramount law. Its object is not to grant legislative power, but to confine and restrain it. Without the constitutional limitations, the power to make laws would be absolute.'" This clear distinction suggests to us that the State Legislatures, inheriting the paramount power of the people, need stricter limitations than the Federal Congress, which acts only by virtue of granted powers. On the other hand, the State Executive can be safely trusted with much broader powers than the President, because he is only a local officer; his term is generally shorter than the President's; he is more directly responsible to the people, and if his powers are found by experience to be too full, it is comparatively easy to amend the Constitution from which he derives them. His administration may be corrupt or inefficient, but would never be fatal to the liberties of the people, for he is restrained by the Constitution of the United States, which guarantees republican government and the equality of all men before the law. But the President of the United States, controlling the military power of the country, and backed by an army of 100,000 civil officers, wields a power which menaces the liberties of the people, unless controlled by a faithful Judiciary, and, above all, by a watchful Congress. His influence is not to be measured by the boundaries of the Federal power as expressed in the Constitution. His army of civil officers often gives him almost absolute control of State politics. He may enter a State, and control its political action, manage its conventions and dictate its local nominations, as we have too often seen done. His power is tremendous, and our safety lies in the shortness of his term and the jealousy and watchfulness of Congress.

Government by parties, which has become the form of our political life, has, however, brought one dangerous feature of legislative encroachment, the right claimed by Congress to determine the validity of the electoral vote of any State in a Presidential election. We have had one narrow escape from civil war through this source. Such a contingency may never arise again, but so great a peril must be guarded against. If Congress can by this means make a President, the system so carefully devised to maintain the independence of the Executive is broken down, and we are drifting upon the shoals so much feared by the fathers of the Constitution. The same spirit which is always ready to unseat a member in a nearly balanced House of Representatives, for the purpose of increasing the working majority of the party, would not scruple in a closely contested Presidential election to grasp at any technicality to win the grander prize, the control of the Federal Government. These fears may never be realized, but they threaten the most serious invasion of the independence of the Executive ever yet attempted.

If we pass by these dangers as belonging to the future rather than the past, we may conclude, as the result of our inquiry into the changes in the Federal Government, that there has been no great alteration in the relative powers of Congress and the President since 1789. The bold position assumed by Jackson was abandoned by his successors, and the power of appointment and removal which he wielded with such success, the later Presidents have been compelled to surrender or share with their political supporters in Congress. In this respect and in some others Congress has encroached somewhat upon the powers formerly possessed by the President, but there has been no material change.

V.

THE JUDICIARY.

So far our attention has been mainly occupied with the struggles for power between what may be called the two great political departments of the State, those who make the laws and those who execute them, and the efforts of the people to curb them both. The relations of each of these powers to the Judiciary, the interpreters of the law, now remain to be considered, and it will be clearly seen that the Courts have increased steadily in power and independence, so far as their relations to the two co-ordinate branches of government are concerned. This steady growth of the authority of the Judiciary is, to my mind, the most remarkable and unique feature in the history of our system of government. Fifty years ago the power of the Courts excited the wonder of De Tocqueville, and the lapse of time since then has only increased the marvel. The change has been silent but steady; being outside the storms of active politics, it has been little observed and little spoken of, but it has certainly transformed the governments within themselves, and to the Federal Union it has furnished the main bulwark of its power. If there be an essential difference between our system and the other popular governments of the world, it lies in the unusual authority given to the Courts. The changes resulting in this increase of judicial authority I will now trace: first considering the method of appointment of the Judges and their tenure of office; and to avoid repetition, wherever the Judges are spoken of, unless otherwise qualified, the word will be understood to mean the highest Court, the Court of last resort, whether of Colony, State or United States.

Referring to what has already been said of the colonies, it will be remembered that they were classed under three forms of government; seven were Royal Provinces, three were Proprietaries and three were Charter Governments. In the Provinces the King named the Governor, and the Governor appointed the Judges. In the Proprietary Governments the proprietors were the feudal representatives of the King, and they or the Governors chosen by them named the Judges. Under the Charters, in Massachusetts the Governor appointed the Judges, while in Rhode Island and Connecticut they were chosen by the Legislatures. In some of the colonies the Governor's nomination required confirmation by the Council, but, as that body was generally named by the Governor, it altered the case but little. The Judges usually held office for life, but in every colony the Crown claimed the right, as a Court of last resort, to receive appeals from the Colonial Courts. It will be readily seen that where the King, or his direct representative, appointed the Judges, and at the same time exercised an appellate jurisdiction over all their decisions, both the power and the independence of the Judges were much circumscribed.

The Revolutionary Constitutions.

In the Constitutions formed during the Revolution for the government of the infant States, the Legislative branch, as already stated, swallowed up the power of the Executive. In pursuance of the same trend of popular policy, the Legislatures in most of the States controlled the appointment of the Judges. In six States, Connecticut, Rhode Island, New Jersey, Virginia, North Carolina and South Carolina, the Legislature appointed the Judges directly; in four States, New Hampshire, Massachusetts, Pennsylvania and Maryland, they were appointed by the Governor, with the consent of the Council; in New York, by the Governor, with the consent of a special council chosen by the Legislature from their own number solely to supervise the appointments of officers; in Delaware, by the Executive and Legislature; but in Georgia they were chosen by popular election, the first instance probably in America of an elective Judiciary. The Judges could everywhere be impeached for misdemeanor by the lower house of the Legislature, and tried by the upper. In addition to this, in five States they could be removed by the Governor, on an address from both branches of the Legislature, a provision retained in many State Constitutions to-day.

Besides this control over the Judiciary, the Legislatures of five States, Rhode Island, Connecticut, New York, New Jersey and South Carolina, exercised distinct judicial functions apart from the usual right of trying impeachments. This practice took different forms in different States, usually the upper house, together with either the Governor or Lieutenant-Governor, sat as a Chancery Court or as a Court of Appeals. In Delaware, on the other hand, while the Legislature exercised no judicial functions, the Chief Executive, called the President, was ex-officio a member of the Court of Appeals. This confusion of duties has disappeared with a clearer understanding of the bounds of the different departments, and survives nowhere in the United States at present. These early Constitutions provided that the Judges should have adequate salaries, sometimes fixing the amount; two of them providing that their compensation should not be diminished during their term of office, a provision very generally adopted now; but they were left everywhere dependent on a legislative appropriation for their salaries.

In the instruments under review, the Judges usually held office during good behavior; this was certainly so in eight States, New Hampshire, Massachusetts, New York, Delaware, Maryland, Virginia, North Carolina and South Carolina; New York alone retiring them at sixty years of age. In Pennsylvania and New Jersey the term was seven years while in Georgia the Judges were chosen by the people every year. In Rhode Island and Connecticut, according to Bancroft, they were appointed by the Legislature annually. The Judges were usually forbidden to hold other offices, especially of a legislative character, which is a very common prohibition in modern constitutions.

Modern Constitutions.

The experience of a century under written constitutions has led our people to a constantly clearer perception of the natural boundaries of the three co-ordinate powers of government, and a constantly sharper limitation of their functions, each to its own field. The Legislature has been shorn of its unjust supremacy and confined to its rightful limits; the power of the Executive has been restored to a proper degree, and the judicial powers of the Legislature, except the trial of impeachments, have been placed in the hands of the Judges, where they belong, making the balance of power in the State Constitutions far more perfect to-day than ever before.

At the same time the people by a natural jealousy have taken into their own hands the power of choosing their officers, which before they had delegated to their representatives. The Governors are no longer chosen by the Legislatures, but by the people. The Judges are no longer chosen by the Legislatures nor appointed by the Governors, but in twenty-six States they are elected directly by the people. The twelve exceptions are as follows: In Delaware the Governor appoints; in Massachusetts and New Hampshire the Governor with the consent of the Council; in Florida, Georgia, Mississippi, Louisiana and New Jersey, the Governor with the consent of the Senate; in Connecticut, Rhode Island, South Carolina and Virginia, the Legislature elects. It will be noticed that these are all old States, though in some cases under new Constitutions. The only States retaining the tenure during good behavior are New Hampshire (limited to seventy years of age), Massachusetts, Delaware, Florida and Rhode Island; in the last named State the Judges holding office till the place is declared vacant by a majority of the Legislature. In the remaining thirty-three States the term is fixed, running from two years in Vermont to twenty-one in Pennsylvania, the average term being eight and one-half years, though in New Hampshire, Connecticut and Maryland the tenure of office ceases at seventy years of age. Public opinion seems of late to lean towards longer terms. In Pennsylvania the Judges are not re-eligible, and in Michigan, Ohio, Nevada and California they are not eligible for any except judicial offices during the term for which they were elected. If the Judiciary ought to be independent of politics, this is certainly a wise provision. It will perhaps surprise the casual reader to learn that in thirty States the Judges may be removed by the Legislature, or by the Governor on an address from the Legislature, which usually requires two-thirds of each House. This is independent of the right of impeachment, which prevails in every State except Oregon.

So much for the methods of appointment and the tenure of office. The tendency is certainly towards placing the Judges on a footing independent of the other departments of the Government, and directly dependent upon the people. Whether an elective Judiciary is an improvement on the old methods of appointment, is a mooted question; but one thing is certain, no inclination is manifested by the people to return to the old-fashioned method of appointment in those States where the Judges are chosen directly by popular vote. There is, however, a decided leaning towards longer terms of office for Judges in the States; and a longer tenure of office with more adequate compensation would certainly go a long way towards correcting any alleged deterioration in the quality of the elective Judiciary.

The direct relations of the Bench to the Executive will next occupy our attention, and after that the power assumed by American Judges to declare a statute to be in conflict with the Constitution.

Relations of the Judiciary to the Executive.

The power of the Judiciary to control the action of the co-ordinate powers of the Government, especially the Executive, either by mandamus or injunction, involves some of the most delicate and difficult questions in the machinery of our governments. Most of the cases concern its relations to the Executive, and the Courts, with admirable discretion, have tried to steer clear of a collision with the rival authorities.

"In many cases," says Justice Story, "the decisions of the Executive and Legislative Departments become final and conclusive—being from their very nature and character incapable of revision. Thus, in measures exclusively of a political, executive or legislative character, it is plain that as the supreme authority as to these questions belongs to the Executive and Legislative Departments, they cannot be re-examined elsewhere."

As early as 1802, the Federal Courts, in Marbury's case, laid down the rule that "questions in their nature political, or which are by the Constitution and laws submitted to the Executive, can never be made in this Court." Johnston's Political Cyclopedia cites several unsuccessful attempts to involve the President and the Supreme Court in conflicts of authority. In 1807 an effort was made to compel the personal attendance of the President as a witness in Burr's case, but it did not succeed. In 1861 the Chief Justice ordered an attachment to issue against an army officer for disregarding the writ of habeas corpus which had been suspended, but when the attachment was returned unsatisfied, the Chief Justice abandoned all proceedings. In October, 1865, and until martial law had ceased in the South, the Court refused to hold sessions in that section. In 1867 the State of Mississippi applied to the Supreme Court for an injunction forbidding the President to execute the Reconstruction Acts, but the injunction was refused. In this case Chief Justice Chase said: "The Congress is the Legislative Department of the Government; the President is the Executive Department; neither can be restrained in its action by the Judicial Department, though the acts of both when performed are, in proper cases, subject to its cognizance." The "proper cases" are such as are not political in their nature.

But while the Courts will not interfere in cases of a purely political nature, whatever that may mean, they claim the right to compel the performance by the Executive of duties of a purely ministerial character. The position is thus stated by

Chancellor Kent: "The principle settled in Marbury's case was that the official acts of the heads of the Executive Department as organs of the President, which are of a political nature, and rest under the Constitution and laws, in Executive discretion, are not within judicial cognizance. But when duties are imposed upon such heads, affecting the rights of individuals, and which the President cannot lawfully forbid—as for instance, to record a patent, or furnish a copy of a record,—the person in that case is the officer of the law and amenable thereto in the ordinary course of justice." This power of the Courts to compel the performance of an act merely ministerial in its nature was denied by President Jefferson, but it has been repeatedly affirmed by the Supreme Court, and acquiesced in as established law. In Kendall's case it was decided by the Supreme Court of the United States that the Circuit Court of the District of Columbia had authority to issue and enforce obedience to a mandamus requiring the performance of a mere ministerial act by the Postmaster-General, which neither he nor the President had any authority to deny or control; for the Postmaster-General is not subject to the direction and control of the President with respect to the execution of duties imposed on him by law. The President has no dispensing power over the law. And more recently, in *The United States* v. *Schurz*, the Secretary of the Interior was compelled by mandamus to deliver a patent for lands to the relator. There are many other cases in which the same doctrine has been affirmed in the Federal Courts.

With respect to the Executive officers of the States there is a difference of opinion, the Courts being about equally divided. In several of the States a mandamus will lie to compel performance of purely ministerial duties by the Executive, while in others it has been thought to be subversive of the balance between the three great departments.

INTERFERENCE WITH THE INDEPENDENCE OF THE COURTS.

It might be expected in the violent changes of political complexion constantly occurring in our governments, that the other departments must sometimes be tempted to lay hands upon the Judiciary, and try to mould it to their purposes, but such instances are rare. This is remarkable, for the Courts inevitably reflect to a certain extent the dominant public sentiment in their decisions, as for example, the strong centralizing drift of the Federal Courts in the time of the first Presidents, the Dred Scott decision under Taney, and the Granger cases of 1876. And when that sentiment changes, and Congress and the President find themselves representing a public feeling and a public policy at variance with the Courts, as was the case under Jefferson and his immediate successors, and again under Lincoln, we might reasonably look for some effort to control its action, but the Courts are so strongly intrenched behind their constitutional independence that very few assaults have been made upon them.

In 1801, at the expiration of the Presidential term of Adams, a system of sixteen Federal Circuit Courts was established by Congress, and the Judgeships were filled by men of the Federal party. Great indignation was expressed that these appointments were made at the very close of Adams' term, and the appointees were nicknamed the "Midnight Judges," because it was said that Adams signed their commissions at midnight of his last day in office. Party feeling ran so high that at the next session of Congress, Jefferson being President, the Courts were abolished and the "Midnight Judges" were ousted.

Very shortly after this, in 1804, an effort was made to remove Judge Chase, one of the Associate Justices of the United States Supreme Court, by impeachment, but he was acquitted in the Senate, although a majority voted for conviction on some of the charges. The motive of this attack was political and the vote on the charges divided mainly on party lines.

In 1866, during President Johnson's term, Congress reduced the number of Justices on the Supreme Bench from ten to seven, to prevent his filling the vacancies with his political friends. By the statute of 1863 the Court was composed of a Chief Justice and nine Associate Justices. Justice Catron died in 1865, and Congress passed the singular statute alluded to above, providing that "no vacancy in the office of Associate Justice of the Supreme Court shall be filled by appointment until the number of Associate Justices shall be reduced to six, and thereafter the said Supreme Court shall consist of a Chief Justice and six Associate Justices," etc. Justice Wayne died in July, 1867, and Justice Grier resigned in February, 1869, reducing the Court to the statutory number of seven. Grant was inaugurated President March 4, 1869, and in April of the same year Congress raised the number of Associate Justices to eight, one less than under the statute of 1863, and Bradley and Strong were appointed to the vacancies. These appear to be the only instances in which Congress has interfered with the Federal Courts.

The President, however, has a direct influence on the Bench in his power of appointment to vacancies, which he always fills with men in sympathy with his own political views. In this way the political complexion of the Court is constantly changing. But it should be said that though many appointments have been made of men active in politics, as, for example, Taney and Chase, no stain has ever been cast upon the integrity or honesty of their decisions after being placed upon the Bench. Probably the most remarkable instance of a change in the tone of the Court brought about by new appointments, was regarding the Legal Tender Question. In 1869 the Court held, five to three, that United States notes were not a legal tender for debts existing before the passage of the law of 1862. In 1871 the Court reversed this decision, by five to four, having in the meantime received two new Judges, Bradley and Strong.

The limits of this paper forbid any extended examination of the relations of the Judiciary in the State Governments to the other departments. In the early years of the republic there was undoubtedly a much greater jealousy on the part of the State Legislatures towards the Courts than exists to-day, and a much stronger inclination to interfere with them on political grounds.

I have only room to mention a few prominent instances. In Pennsylvania, in 1804, after a political revolution at the polls, Judge Addison, President Judge of the Court of Common Pleas for the Western District of the State, was impeached and removed from office by a strict party vote; and an attempt was made to remove from the Bench by impeachment Judges of the Supreme Court of the State, which failed, although a majority of the Senators voted for it.

In 1856, Judge Woodbury Davis of the Supreme Court of Maine was impeached and removed by a party vote, and the office which he held was abolished. A year later, a revolution having taken place in the politics of the State, the office was re-established and Judge Davis was re-appointed. In 1858, the Massachusetts Legislature by address requested the Governor to remove Judge Loring from the Bench on political grounds, but the Governor refused.

Other instances of attacks by the Legislatures of different States upon their Judges for political reasons will be mentioned later, when treating of the resistance made by the Legislatures to the claims of the Courts. Such cases have occurred mainly in periods of unusual political excitement and are growing more and more rare. It has already been shown that in nearly every State the Supreme Court has been placed by the Constitution on an independent footing, and apparently there is little disposition at the present time to interfere with the inferior Courts for selfish or political ends.

Great Power of American Courts.

We have seen in the course of this sketch the most radical changes in the relations of the three co-ordinate powers of Government. The Executive, all-powerful at the beginning, was reduced to a mere shadow of its former glory, and in these later days is regaining some of its lost power. The Legislature, at first weak, afterwards absorbed the powers of the other departments, but is now much reduced again. Throughout all these changes the dignity and power of the Judges have steadily increased. Their independence has been spoken of, and their claim to control even the conduct of the Executive in purely ministerial acts, but their greatest power, most amazing to Europeans, is the authority to set aside a statute which they hold to be in conflict with the written Constitution. No other Courts in the world possess this unique power. The Supreme Courts of the States may pronounce upon the constitutionality of the statutes of the State Legislature, while the Supreme Court of the United States may sit in judgment upon the laws of Congress, the official acts of the President to a certain extent, upon the statutes of the States, nay, even upon the State Constitutions themselves. "The Supreme Court," said De Tocqueville, "is placed higher than any known tribunal, both by the nature of its rights and the class of justiciable parties which it controls."

This increase of the judicial power in America results, first, from the steady growth of the idea that the Constitution, the fundamental law of the State, should be an instrument emanating directly from the people, and controlling the acts of the Government instituted under it; next, as the natural corollary of this, it was recognized that the power must lie somewhere to compare the acts of the Executive and Legislature with the Constitution, and it could only lie properly in the Courts.

We are so accustomed to-day to the machinery of a Constitutional Convention, chosen solely to frame a government, and when it has completed its work, submitting the instrument to ratification by popular vote, that we forget there was a time when these forms were new, a time when the Legislatures claimed these powers, and made and unmade Constitutions. Our Revolutionary fathers were colonial Englishmen before they were Americans, and they inherited the love for English institutions and that reverence for Parliament which clothes it with absolute power. So in the early days of the Revolution, we find our Legislatures claiming the same wide stretch of authority that belonged to the British Parliament. When the Colonies, in 1775 and 1776, threw off the yoke of Great Britain, it was in every case an act of the Legislature, and in no instance were the people consulted directly. The new forms of government then adopted were not submitted to direct ratification by popular vote, except in New Hampshire and Massachusetts. In Rhode Island and Connecticut the Legislatures simply declared their independence, and re-affirmed the forms of government already existing under their charters. In South Carolina, a Constitution was framed and adopted by the Legislature; while two years later, in 1778, the same body by a mere statute repealed this fundamental instrument and adopted a new one. In Virginia a Convention composed of 45 members of the House of Burgesses framed and adopted a Constitution which stood till 1830. In Delaware, Georgia, Maryland, New Hampshire, New Jersey, New York, North Carolina and Pennsylvania, Conventions elected for the purpose framed and adopted Constitutions. In Massachusetts alone, the work of the Convention was submitted to the people for ratification, which took place in 1780. In Delaware, Georgia, New Hampshire and Pennsylvania, new Constitutions, to supersede the temporary instruments first adopted, were framed by Conventions within a few years, but only in New Hampshire was it thought necessary to ratify the work of the Convention by popular vote.

The object of entering thus into detail on this point was to show the growth of the idea that the Constitution is the direct legislative act of the people, and that as such it must of course control any acts of their agents, the Legislature; for on this point rests the tremendous power exercised by the American Judiciary to declare laws unconstitutional. Of course the authority to compare this fundamental instrument with the statutes enacted by the Legislature meeting under it, can lie in the Judicial Department only.

This idea of a power overriding the statute of the Legislature was not wholly new to the colonists. Professor Dicey, in a recent article in the *English Law Quarterly Review*, speaking to this point, says: "To any one who had inhabited a colony governed under a charter, the effect of which on the validity of a colonial law was certainly liable to be considered by the Privy Council, there was nothing startling in empowering the Judiciary to pronounce in given cases upon the constitutionality of acts passed by assemblies whose powers were limited by the Constitution, just as the authority of the colonial legislatures was limited by charter or by Act of Parliament." The origin and growth of this power is ably treated by Mr. Brooks Adams in the *Atlantic Monthly*, November, 1884.

Resistance to the Claims of the Courts.

This claim of authority was not, however, surrendered to the Courts without a struggle. In 1786, the Supreme Court of Rhode Island pronounced an act passed by the Legislature to be in conflict with the Colonial Charter which had then become the Constitution of the State. This case is peculiarly interesting as one of the first instances in which a legislative enactment was declared void on the ground of incompatibility with a State Constitution. The next Legislature refused to re-elect these Judges when their terms expired at the end of the year, and filled their places with men more in harmony with the Legislature.

In 1820 Webster made an appeal to the Massachusetts Constitutional Convention in behalf of an independent Judiciary, and in opposition to a proposed amendment whereby the Governor might remove Judges on an address from a bare majority of the Legislature. During his argument, he said that if the records of neighboring States were examined, "it might be found that cases had happened in which laws known to be at best very questionable as to their consistency with the Constitution had been passed, and at the same session, effectual measures taken under the power of removal by address, to create a new Bench." We have no means of knowing to what State he referred, as he cited no instances; but the practice had evidently been common enough to excite his alarm, and that the Legislatures should have recourse to this indirect method of impeachment in order to maintain their authority, and even anticipate an adverse decision by removal of the obnoxious Judges, shows how reluctant they were to submit to restraint.

But the most remarkable struggle took place in Ohio in 1807, where a Circuit Judge declared a law unconstitutional, and on appeal his decision was sustained by a majority of the Supreme Court of the State. Upon this the Circuit Judge and the two members of the Supreme Court sustaining his decision were impeached by the lower house of the Legislature, and actually brought to trial for daring to declare a statute unconstitutional. They were not, however, convicted. The right to pronounce a law void from incompatibility with the Constitution was asserted by the Supreme Court of the United States for the first time in the great case of *Marbury* v. *Madison* in 18c2. The same ground had been previously taken by the Federal Circuit Courts as early as 1797, and by the Supreme Courts of some of the States.

In the heat of great political excitement the question has been sometimes raised, how far the decision of the Supreme Court of the United States on the constitutionality of a measure is binding as a precedent upon Congress and the

President. Jefferson, who was jealous of the claims of the Court, says in his correspondence: "My construction is that each department of the government is truly independent of the others, and has an equal right to decide for itself what is the meaning of the Constitution in the laws submitted to its action, and especially when it is to act ultimately and without appeal." He then proceeds to give examples in which he disregarded, when President, the decisions of the Judiciary, and refers to the Alien and Sedition Laws, and the case of *Marbury* v. *Madison*. Jackson made the same claim in his famous Veto Message, in even stronger language, which has already been quoted. Lincoln alluded to it in his first inaugural, referring to the Dred Scott case, which affirmed the right of the slave-holder to hold his slaves in the Territories; and during Johnson's impeachment trial his counsel, especially Mr. Evarts and Mr. Stanbery, re-asserted the doctrine in its full force. Jackson's position was opposed with great earnestness by Madison in his correspondence, and by Webster in his famous speech upon the Veto of the Bank Bill. It may safely be said that to-day the doctrine is abandoned, and is not likely ever to appear again, unless in the furnace of extreme political heat, when the passions of men warp and twist everything to their purposes.

The scope of this power to declare a law unconstitutional is much broadened by the modern tendency to limit legislation, which has already been spoken of. The early Constitutions were very brief, containing usually little more than a bill of rights and a skeleton of the government, leaving all details to the discretion of the Legislature. Now all this is changed, the bounds of the different departments are carefully defined, and the power of the Legislature is jealously curbed, particularly in the domain of special legislation. It will be seen at a glance that this enlarges the relative power of the Courts. It limits the Legislature, and widens the field of the Judiciary at one stroke.

What, then, is the sum of our examination regarding the Judiciary? History teaches that it has grown steadily in importance during the entire century. This change is both safe and wise; because the Courts are the weakest of the three departments; they hold neither the purse nor the sword; they have no patronage to dispense; their power is passive rather than active, and in case of resistance to their decrees, they must depend on the other departments to give them vitality. If at any time they show an inclination to abuse their power, the right of impeachment still remains, and behind that the right of removal in most of the States. There can be little danger, then, from this increase in the authority of the Judges; it has strengthened the weak and not the strong, and made a juster and more even balance of power between the three branches of government.

CONCLUSION.

We have passed in review the drift of popular opinion on these subjects, as crystallized into institutions, during a period reaching back into colonial times. In the State governments we have seen the Governor, once the august symbol of royalty, shorn of his strength and reduced to a mere shadow of power; then later still, by a reaction, endowed again with much of his original authority. We have seen the Legislature, at first weak and limited, spring, at one bound, under the stimulus of a revolt against royal oppression, almost into the omnipotence of a British Parliament; then afterwards, gradually stripped of its greatness, cramped and fettered in its movements by a revulsion of popular sentiment, which singularly enough shows a greater distrust of the legislators, the popular body, than of either Governor or Judges. And last of all, the authority of the Judiciary, both Federal and State, has constantly increased throughout the century. We, as Americans, do not feel its influence, for we are used to it from childhood, but the foreigner who comes fresh to the study of our institutions is amazed at its extent, and at the reverence with which our people submit to the decrees of the

Courts, even the sovereign States bowing their heads in submission. The century has wrought marvelous changes in our country, in its breadth, in its nearness to the old world, in the character of its people, in the power of the Federal Government, and in its relation to the States; but with all these changes, the type of popular government has drawn nearer and nearer to the ideal of a perfect balance of co-ordinate powers.

Looking back over the whole field, the points that have surprised and impressed me are the distrust and consequent depression of the legislative power in the States, and the steady elevation of the Judiciary, in both State and Federal Governments. The first surprised me, for I had been told so often the voice of the people was the voice of God that such a distrust seemed at first almost like a confession of failure of popular government; but may we not more justly say it is a mark of wisdom in the people, that, knowing their own passions and frailties, they guard against them by putting bits in the mouths of their own representatives? On the other hand, while doing this, they have enlarged the field of the Judges, who represent the deeper and more abiding popular sense of order and justice; that stream of feeling which flows with steady volume, deep and strong, hardly moved by those tempests of popular fury which lash the surface for a time and then as rapidly subside. The Court is the instrument of the people no less than the Legislature; but it represents the popular sentiment in a deeper, calmer, more lasting form, and embodies their aspirations after an ideal of perfect order; the law expresses the conscience of the people.

The Courts the Conscience of the People.

Why, then, should the Judiciary so often be excepted when we speak of popular institutions? It is sometimes spoken of as though it were almost antagonistic to the people. Possibly this arises from the fact that the law is the field occupied exclusively by a separate guild of men, whom De Tocqueville terms the only real aristocracy in America. Possibly it is because the function of the Court is so often to bring back the people from a state of excitement and fury to a calm sense of right. But whatever may be the causes of this sentiment, it has no ground in fact. The Judiciary is as really a part of the people's government as any department. The interpretation of the law represents the popular sentiment of order and justice as fully as the written statute. The Court can go no farther towards absolute right than it is sustained by popular opinion, and its decisions must represent the average public sentiment; not the froth and fury of a political campaign, but the calm, settled conviction of thinking men. If the popular conscience is quickened, the judicial interpretation, as well as the statutes, must reflect its increased sensitiveness, and it, too, becomes more liberal and humane. So that to clothe the Courts with these unusual powers indicates no distrust of democratic institutions, but rather an appeal from the passions to the better judgment, to the calm conscience of the people.

This exaltation of the Judiciary in our scheme of government should excite our patriotic pride, for it is a positive advance in the art of government. We may justly lay a bolder claim, and say it marks a higher civilization, a reverence for law itself as above the men who make the statute or those who are the instruments of its execution. In the simpler and ruder forms of government the Executive absorbs the other powers. The despotic autocrat makes the laws, interprets, and executes them. As the world advances and the nations become more enlightened, the people claim a share in the public affairs; this idea culminates in the supremacy of the Parliament, where both Executive and Judiciary may be made and unmade at the will of the popular body. Our own country, in its brief history, has passed through both these stages. The colonial period was marked by the overshadowing power of the Executive;

while at a later stage, in the heat of the Revolution, the temper of our people would bear nothing short of the absolute supremacy of the Legislature. But the ripened fruit of our experience is this modern idea of government, which lifts up the Judiciary to an exalted and independent position, and places law, impersonal, impassive, and serene, in the innermost shrine of the temple, jealously guarded from profane intrusion.

What confidence this inspires in the wisdom and integrity of human nature, in the power of the people for self-government! A century of experience, checkered by foreign and domestic wars, with marvelous growth of power and wealth, ends in a more perfect realization of the type of popular government. A century of various trials leads to the elevation of the Judiciary, the conscience of the people, for the first time in the history of the world, to its true place as an independent, co-ordinate department of the government.

We have not fully realized our ideal. Our forms are in many respects crude; our practice under them is blurred by the imperfections belonging to human nature; but the grand plan has been outlined, and we are struggling to its attainment. Incomplete as it is, it stands in unique majesty, as the outline of perfect human government, culminating neither in the selfish will of the autocrat, nor in the turbulent ambition of a popular body,—but where the calm majesty of law crowns the great work.

APPENDIX.

TABULATED COMPARISON OF MODERN STATE CONSTITUTIONS.

The following tables are intended to show at a glance the limitations placed upon the power of the different departments of government in the various State Constitutions as now existing. They are necessarily imperfect, for my aim is only to show the salient points of difference. It would need a volume to display the amazing variety of provisions found in all the thirty-eight instruments. The tables fail to show the progress of the science of Constitution-making, because most of the early instruments have been much altered by amendments, and in the tables no discrimination is made between the originals and the amendments. Thus Vermont has recently grafted biennial sessions and an elective Judiciary upon one of the most venerable of State Constitutions (1793); and New York has lately added to that of 1846 very stringent provisions to prevent special legislation.

The provisions on this subject of special legislation were particularly difficult to classify, as there was every shade of prohibition, from that shown in Delaware and Massachusetts, where the Legislatures still have full power, to that shown in California, where such legislation is forbidden by clauses of a most sweeping character. At last, I gave up all attempt at details, and grouped the States in three classes as well as I could—those with full provisions, those with partial prohibition, and those with no provision at all, or very nearly none.

The limitations of the length of sessions are almost as difficult to classify. Seven States absolutely limit the period; thus, Louisiana provides that all legislation after a certain time shall be null and void. Four others, like Georgia, provide a term beyond which it cannot be extended, unless by a two-thirds or three-fifths vote. Virginia, in such cases, forbids an extension of more than thirty days. Missouri and Texas reduce the pay of members after a certain period. Again, five others, like California, cut off their pay entirely. New Jersey, alone, provides a fixed salary of five hundred dollars, without limitation of time.

Regarding the Judiciary, I would add that the Judges can be removed by impeachment, besides the methods mentioned in the tables, in every State, except Oregon, where there seems to be no impeachment.

It is the Louisiana Constitution of 1868 which is analyzed in the tables; with this exception, all the instruments there represented are the very latest adopted.

EXECUTIVE.

	Constitution Adopted.	Length of Term in Years.	Governor's Successor in Case of Vacancy.	Governor has Pardoning Power.*	Number required to over-ride Veto.	Governor may veto items in Appropriation Bills.	Number of days allowed after adjournment for Governor to consider Bills.	Additional Provisions. (See explanation at foot of page.)
Alabama..........	1875	2	Pr. Sen.	*	Majority	*	....	
Arkansas..........	1874	2	Pr. Sen.	*	Majority	*	20	
California..........	1879	4	Lt. Gov.	*	2/3	*	10	
Colorado...	1876	2	Lt. Gov.	*	2/3	*	30	
Connecticut........	1818	1	Lt. Gov.	None.	Majority	......	....	*a*
Delaware..........	1831	4	Sp. Sen.	*	No Veto	......	....	*b*
Florida.............	1868	4	Lt. Gov.	Limited	2/3	*	10	
Georgia...........	1868	4	Pr. Sen.	*	2/3	*	....	
Illinois.............	1870	4	Lt. Gov.	*	2/3	......	10	
Indiana.............	1851	4	Lt. Gov.	Limited	Majority	......	5	*c a*
Iowa...............	1857	2	Lt. Gov.	*	2/3	......	30	
Kansas.............	1859	2	Lt. Gov.	*	2/3	......	....	
Kentucky..........	1850	4	Lt. Gov.	Limited	Majority	......	....	*c*
Louisiana..........	1868	4	Lt. Gov.	*	2/3	......	5	*c d*
Maine...............	1820	1	Lt. Gov.	*	2/3	......	3	*e*
Maryland..........	1867	4	Pr. Sen.	*	3/5	......	....	*f*
Massachusetts....	1780	1	Lt. Gov.	Limited	2/3	......	....	*e*
Michigan...........	1850	2	Lt. Gov.	*	2/3	......	5	
Minnesota.........	1857	2	Lt. Gov.	*	2/3	......	3	
Mississippi........	1868	4	Lt. Gov.	*	2/3	......	†	
Missouri...........	1875	4	Lt. Gov.	*	2/3	*	30	
Nebraska..........	1875	2	Lt. Gov.	*	3/5	*	5	
Nevada............	1864	4	Lt. Gov.	Limited	2/3	......	10	*d*
New Hampshire.	1792	2	Lt. Gov.	Limited	2/3	......	....	*e*
New Jersey........	1844	3	Lt. Gov.	Limited	Majority	*	....	*g*
New York..........	1846	3	Lt. Gov.	*	2/3	*	30	
North Carolina...	1876	4	Lt. Gov.	*	No Veto	......	....	
Ohio................	1851	2	Lt. Gov.	*	No Veto	......	....	
Oregon.............	1857	4	Sec. St.	*	2/3	......	5	*d h*
Pennsylvania......	1873	4	Lt. Gov.	Limited	2/3	*	30	
Rhode Island.....	1842	1	Lt. Gov.	*	No Veto	......	....	
South Carolina....	1868	2	Lt. Gov.	*	2/3	......	....	*d*
Tennessee.........	1870	2	Sp. Sen.	*	Majority	......	....	*i*
Texas..............	1876	2	Lt. Gov.	*	2/3	*	20	
Vermont...........	1793	2	Lt. Gov.	Limited	Majority	......	....	
Virginia...........	1870	4	Lt. Gov.	*	2/3	......	....	*c*
West Virginia....	1872	4	Pr. Sen.	*	Majority	*	5	*c*
Wisconsin.........	1848	2	Lt. Gov.	*	2/3	......	....	

EXPLANATION OF REFERENCES.

(*a*) Legislature only can pardon.
(*b*) Governor not re-eligible; can be removed by two-thirds of each house of Legislature.
(*c*) Governor ineligible for four years from close of term.
(*d*) Bills vetoed after adjournment sent to next session of the Legislature.
(*e*) Executive Council.
(*f*) In case of death, Legislature elects successor.
(*g*) Governor ineligible for three years from close of term.
(*h*) Governor eligible only 8 in 12 years.
(*i*) Governor eligible only 6 years in 8.
† 3 days of next session of Legislature.

LEGISLATURE.

	Constitution Adopted.	Length of Term in Years. Upper House.	Lower House.	Biennial or Annual Sessions.	Restrictions upon Legislation. Limitation of Session, in days.	(*a*) Special Sessions confined to subjects mentioned in call.	(*b*) Bills must be read three separate days.	(*c*) Bills must contain only one subject; expressed in title.	(*d*) Gen'l or Salary Appr'n Bills must contain nothing else.	(*e*) No act can be amen'd by title, full text must be quoted.	(*f*) Bills must be passed by majority of members elect, voting by Ayes and Noes.	Provisions forbidding Special Legislation.
Alabama	1875	4	2	Bien	50	*a*	*b*	*c*	*d*	*e*		Full.
Arkansas	1874	4	2	Bien		*a*	*b*		*d*	*e*	*f*	Full.
California	1879	4	2	Bien	60	*a*	*b*	*c*		*e*	*f*	Full.
Colorado	1876	4	2	Bien	40	*a*	*b*	*c*	*d*	*e*	*f*	Full.
Connecticut	1818	1	1	Ann								None.
Delaware	1831	4	2	Bien								None.
Florida	1868	4	2	Bien	60	*a*	*b*	*c*	*d*	*e*		Full.
Georgia	1868	4	2	Ann	40		*b*	*c*		*e*		Partial.
Illinois	1870	4	2	Bien			*b*	*c*	*d*	*e*	*f*	Full.
Indiana	1851	4	2	Bien	61		*b*	*c*		*e*	*f*	Full.
Iowa	1857	4	2	Bien				*c*			*f*	Full.
Kansas	1859	4	2	Ann	50		*b*	*c*		*e*	*f*	Partial.
Kentucky	1850	4	2	Bien	60		*b*	*c*				Partial.
Louisiana	1868	4	2	Ann	60		*b*			*e*		Partial.
Maine	1820	1	1	Ann								Partial.
Maryland	1867	4	2	Bien	90		*b*	*c*		*e*	*f*	Full.
Massachusetts	1780	1	1	Ann								None.
Michigan	1850	2	2	Bien		*a*		*c*			*f*	None.
Minnesota	1857	2	1	Ann			*b*	*c*			*f*	None.
Mississippi	1868	4	2	Ann			*b*					Partial.
Missouri	1875	4	2	Bien	70	*a*	*b*	*c*		*e*	*f*	Full.
Nebraska	1875	2	2	Bien			*b*	*c*	*d*	*e*	*f*	Full.
Nevada	1864	4	2	Bien	60	*a*	*b*	*c*		*e*	*f*	Full.
New Hampshire	1792	2	2	Bien						*e*		None.
New Jersey	1844	3	1	Ann		*a*		*c*			*f*	Full.
New York	1846	2	1	Ann				*c*		*e*	*f*	Full.
North Carolina	1876	2	2	Bien	60							Partial.
Ohio	1851	2	2	Bien			*b*	*c*		*e*	*f*	Partial.
Oregon	1857	4	2	Bien	40		*b*	*c*		*e*	*f*	Full.
Pennsylvania	1873	4	2	Bien		*a*	*b*	*c*		*e*	*f*	Full.
Rhode Island	1842	1	1	Ann								None.
South Carolina	1868	4	2	Ann			*b*	*c*				Partial.
Tennessee	1870	2	2	Bien	75		*b*	*c*		*e*	*f*	Full.
Texas	1876	4	2	Bien	60	*a*	*b*	*c*		*e*		Full.
Vermont	1793	2	2	Bien								None.
Virginia	1870	4	2	Bien	90		*b*	*c*		*e*		Partial.
West Virginia	1872	4	2	Bien	45		*b*	*c*		*e*		Full.
Wisconsin	1848	2	1	Ann				*c*				Full.

ADDITIONAL PROVISIONS.

ALABAMA.—All bills must be referred to a committee.

ARKANSAS.—No new bill can be introduced during the last three days of the session.

CALIFORNIA.—All bills must be printed. No new bill can be introduced after 50 days of session, without consent of two-thirds.

COLORADO.—All bills must be considered by a committee and printed. No new bill can be introduced after 25 days of session.

ILLINOIS.—Cumulative voting allowed for Lower House. All bills must be printed.

MARYLAND.—No new bill can be introduced during last ten days of session.

MICHIGAN.—No new bill can be introduced after 50 days of session. Two-thirds vote required to appropriate public money for private purposes.

MINNESOTA.—No bill can be passed on day of adjournment.

MISSISSIPPI.—Ayes and Noes required on all bills appropriating money.

MISSOURI.—All bills must be referred to a committee and printed.

NEBRASKA.—Continuing appropriations forbidden.

NEW YORK.—Private and local bills must contain one subject only, expressed in title.

NORTH CAROLINA.—Bills to impose taxes or contract debts must be read three separate days.

PENNSYLVANIA.—All bills must be referred to a committee and be printed.

TENNESSEE.—Two-thirds required for a quorum. Ayes and Noes required on all bills of a general character and on appropriation bills.

TEXAS.—Two-thirds required for a quorum. All bills must be referred to a committee and reported three days before adjournment.

WISCONSIN.—All bills must be printed. Private and local bills must contain but one subject, expressed in title. Bills to contract debts require a majority of members elect by Ayes and Noes.

JUDICIARY.

	Constitution Adopted.	Length of Term in Years.	By Whom Chosen	By Whom Removable.	Additional Provisions. (See explanat'n at foot of page.)
Alabama	1875	6	People.	Impeachment only.	
Arkansas	1874	8	People.	(Gov'r on address two-thirds each house Legislature.)	
California	1879	12	People.	(Concurrent Vote two-thirds each house Legislature.)	*a b c*
Colorado	1876	9	People.	Impeachment only.	
Connecticut	1818	8	Legislature	As in Arkansas.	*d*
Delaware	1831	Life	Governor.	As in Arkansas.	
Florida	1868	Life	(Gov'r cons't Senate.)	Impeachment only.	
Georgia	1868	12	(Gov'r cons't Senate.)	As in Arkansas.	
Illinois	1870	9	People.	(Concurrent Vote three-quarters each house Legislature.)	
Indiana	1851	6	People.	(Joint Resolution two-thirds each house Legislature.)	
Iowa	1857	6	People.	Impeachment only.	
Kansas	1859	6	People.	As in Indiana.	
Kentucky	1850	8	People.	As in Arkansas.	
Louisiana	1868	8	(Gov'r cons't Senate.)	As in Arkansas.	
Maine	1820	4	People.	(Gov'r on address both houses of Leg'ture, and advice of Council)	
Maryland	1867	15	People.	As in Arkansas.	*d*
Massachusetts	1780	Life	(Gov'r cons't Council.)	(Gov'r on address of both houses of Legislature.)	
Michigan	1850	8	People.	As in Arkansas.	*e*
Minnesota	1857	7	People.	Impeachment only.	
Mississippi	1868	9	(Gov'r cons't Senate.)	As in Arkansas.	
Missouri	1875	10	People.	As in Arkansas.	
Nebraska	1875	6	People.	(Impeachment by Legislature, Trial by District Judges.)	*a*
Nevada	1864	6	People.	As in California.	*b*
New Hampsh'e	1792	Life	(Gov'r cons't Council.)	As in Maine.	*d*
New Jersey	1844	7	(Gov'r cons't Senate.)	Impeachment only.	
New York	1846	14	People.	As in California.	*a d*
North Carolina	1876	8	People.	As in California.	
Ohio	1851	5	People.	As in California.	*b*
Oregon	1857	6	People.	As in Arkansas.	
Pennsylvania	1873	21	People.	As in Arkansas.	*f*
Rhode Island	1842	Life	Legislature	Maj. both houses Leg'ture.	
South Carolina	1868	6	Legislature	As in Arkansas.	
Tennessee	1870	8	People.	As in California.	
Texas	1876	6	People.	As in Arkansas.	
Vermont	1793	2	People.	Impeachment only.	
Virginia	1870	12	Legislature	As in Rhode Island.	
West Virginia	1872	12	People.	As in California.	
Wisconsin	1848	6	People.	As in Arkansas.	

EXPLANATION OF REFERENCES.

(*a*) Judges must not practice law.
(*b*) Ineligible during term except for judicial office.
(*c*) Must render decision in 90 days.
(*d*) Judges retired at 70 years.
(*e*) Judges ineligible, except for judicial office, during term and one year thereafter.
(*f*) Not re-eligible.